Top Notes

Stephen Daldry's
Billy Elliot

Study notes for Standard English:
Module C 2015-2020 HSC

Julia C. Z. Walters

— A —
FIVE SENSES
PUBLICATION

Five Senses Education Pty Ltd
2/195 Prospect Highway
Seven Hills 2147
New South Wales
Australia

Copyright © Five Senses Education Pty Ltd 2008
First Published 2004. This edition 2016.

Walters, Julia,
Top Notes – Billy Elliot
ISBN 978-1-76032-052-2

CONTENTS

INTRODUCTION TO THE TOP NOTES SERIES

This series has been created to assist HSC students of English in their understanding of set texts. Top Notes are easy to read, providing analysis of issues and discussion of important ideas contained in the texts.

Particular care has been taken to ensure that students are able to examine each text in the context of the module and elective to which it has been allocated.

Each text includes:

- Notes on the specific module and elective
- Plot summary
- Character analysis
- Setting
- Thematic concerns
- Language studies
- Essay questions and a response
- Suggested related material if required
- Additional study questions
- Useful quotations

I am sure you will find these Top Notes useful in your studies of English.

Bruce Pattinson
Series Editor

THE STANDARD COURSE

This is a brief analysis of the Standard course to ensure you are completely familiar with what you are attempting in the examination. If in any doubt at all check with your teacher or the Board of Studies.

The Standard Course requires you to have studied:

- Four prescribed texts. This means four texts from the list given to your teacher by the Board of Studies.

- For each of the texts, **one** must come from **each** of the following four categories.
    - drama
    - poetry
    - prose fiction (novel usually)
    - nonfiction or media or film or multimedia texts. (Multimedia are CD ROMs, websites, etc.)

- A range of related texts of your own choosing. These are part of your Area of Study, Module A and Module C. Do not confuse these with the main set text you are studying.

Paper One

Area of Study: Discovery

Paper Two

Module A	Module B	Module C
Experience through Language	**Close Study of Text**	**Texts and Society**
Electives	*Electives*	*Electives*
• Distinctive Voices OR • Distinctively Visual	• Drama OR • Prose Fiction OR • Nonfiction, Film, Media, Multimedia OR • Poetry	• Exploring Interactions OR • Exploring Transitions

You must study the Area of Study and EACH of Modules A, B and C
There are elective and text options within EACH of these that
your school

MODULE C: TEXTS AND SOCIETY

The prescriptions document outlines that this module requires students, 'to explore and analyse texts used in a specific situation'. To explore a text we must critically engage with it. This will require reading, or in this case, viewing, the text more than once. In analysing a text well, critically examine the features of the text in order to explain it and evaluate its effectiveness.

In completing this module, the Board of Studies also expects students understand "the ways that texts communicate information, ideas, bodies of knowledge, attitudes and belief systems in ways particular to specific areas of society" (Refer to the English Stage 6 Syllabus, p 31.)

The ways that texts communicate refers to the language features that are evident within the text. Therefore, you will need to become familiar with all film techniques. Film techniques are the visual and filmic features of film. They are the 'language' of film.

While a solid understanding of language features and film techniques is crucial to success in the HSC, you cannot mention these film techniques on their own. In other words, must do more than simply list film techniques. You need to also explain how the film techniques communicate or represent information and ideologies held by the particular societies within the text. Ideologies are simply the attitudes and the belief systems that belong to a group of people or peoples. For example explore how the techniques used in the film represent the society in *Billy Elliot*, which believes that boys should play rugby or football and ballet should only be performed by girls.

The elective of 'Exploring Transitions', focuses on the specific situation of growing up and transitional phases that people go through to find their own place in the world. You will need to differentiate how individuals experience this growth and change differently. Not only will you use this information to guide your analysis of *Billy Elliot* but you also need to examine and refer to other related texts. Finally, using this information you will respond to and even compose your own texts that actually "demonstrate different pathways to new experiences".

Use the terminology that the Board of Studies uses in the rubric in your own responses and compositions, whether assessment tasks or exam responses. This lets your teacher and examiner know that you are indeed focused and that you are aware of the requirements set by the Board of Studies.

Use the following lists as a guide to words which relate to transitions.

Look up three words in each list which you do not know. Then write in a sentence how the word might relate to the concept of transition.

- Adolescent
- Blossoming
- Burgeoning
- Change
- Developing
- Emergent
- Evolving

- Germinating
- Growing up
- Growth
- Heightening
- Incipient
- Magnifying
- Maturing

- Nascent
- Stage
- Potential
- Pullulating

Knowledge

- Accomplishments
- Awareness
- Axiom
- Cognition
- Comprehension
- Credence
- Deduction

- Discernment
- Erudition
- Ethnology
- Expectation
- Intellect
- Intelligence
- Mores

- Perception
- Perspicacity
- Precipitance
- Realisation
- Supposition
- Surmise
- Thesis

Attitudes and Beliefs

- Angle
- Assumption
- Bias
- Character
- Conviction
- Countenance
- Credence
- Culture
- Demeanour
- Disposition
- Dogma
- Faith
- Hypothesis
- Ideology
- Inclination
- Judgment
- Perspective
- Philosophy
- Predilection
- Principles
- Proclivity

Experiences

- Adventures
- Affair
- Biography
- Encounter
- Episode
- Event
- Exploit
- Feat
- Happening
- Incident
- Memoir
- Occurrence
- Ordeal
- Personal account
- Personal narrative
- Profile
- Reminisces
- Trial
- Venture

IN SUMMARY

This module and elective require you to do the following with the prescribed text, *Billy Elliot* and related material:

- Engage and explore the prescribed text *Billy Elliot*. Focus especially on transitions in an analysis. Consider the changes brought by adolescence and growing up.

- Find other related texts which link to aspects of transition.

- Consider, through textual examples, how different people deal with growth and change.

- Consider transitions in relation to the belief systems and ideologies held by society.

- Consider how belief systems and ideologies are represented in your texts.

- Respond to and compose your own texts that explore transitions. Ensure you employ various techniques relevant to your text type, to explore transitional phases.

STUDYING FILM

Film provides a source of entertainment, even escapism, on a daily basis. Although many films can be enjoyed and interpreted with little effort, others operate on more than one level. As well as entertaining, they have a message for the responder. They tell us something about our world or ourselves.

In order to achieve this level of interpretation, it is essential to consider how film techniques and conventions, the tools of the filmmaker, have been used to make meaning.

We are able to enjoy and understand films everyday because we have an implicit understanding of the basic techniques and conventions upon which a film text relies. For instance, we know that when the camera moves in on a sleeping person's face and the sound becomes distorted and echoing that we are about to see a dream sequence.

Studying film requires a critical awareness of conventions and the technical language, or jargon, required to label and discuss the various components of film. The jargon must be understood in order to analyse how techniques are used by the filmmaker to convey a particular message. The glossary included in this guide provides a basic overview of the terminology required for the study of film as text at HSC level.

It is important to consider that the construction of meaning in film is not accidental, but the result of careful planning. An individual scene in a screenplay will be made up of dozens of individual shots, edited from a much larger amount of raw film footage. In the creation of a shot, the filmmaker considers five variables: shot size, framing, focus, angle and movement. These are the aspects of film language that need to be considered in your analysis and will be discussed in the analysis section of this guide.

In addition, the director gives careful consideration to how each shot is composed. This is called mise-en-scène. Mise-en-scène refers to everything else that happens in a shot, apart from the main action. Analysing this involves looking at elements like setting, costume, lighting and the movements of the other actors in the scene. For instance, costume can be used to convey the social status or personality of a character, lighting can be used to enhance a particular mood or the actions of the main character may contrast to those of other characters in the background of the scene.

The use of sound in a film, including voices, sound effects and the musical score is also an essential consideration. Sound tracks in films are used in two ways. Firstly they include the sounds that we would expect to hear, such as dialogue and realistic sounds like a door closing or the noise of an approaching car. This is called *diegetic* sound because it is part of the narrative. Secondly, the sound track includes sounds that are added to the film to create or suggest certain attitudes or effects – well known songs or an original score may be included to invoke a particular mood or attitude. Exaggerated sound effects and voice overs are other examples. This sound track is called *non-diegetic* sound. Notably, silence is often used as an effective technique and must be considered as part of the sound track.

Finally, it is important to consider the style of the film you are studying, as certain conventions are associated with particular styles and genres of film. *Contact* is an example of science fiction. Events are presented to the viewer, as an observer, in a fantastic way. The technology, off world props, sets and fantasy locations provide a fictional mood for the story.

Steps to follow in the study of a film:

1. Watch the film from beginning to end without interruption, preferably in one sitting.

2. Record your first impressions of the film.

3. Review each sequence of the film, making detailed notes about how the various components of the film have been used by the filmmaker. In this instance, focus on how transitions and societal attitudes have been represented.

4. Create links between the film you have studied and other pieces of related material. Identify similarities and/or differences in terms of the message of the text and/or the language techniques that have been used to convey this message.

5. Tie your ideas together in an extended piece of writing.

GENERAL GLOSSARY OF FILM TERMS

aerial shot

A shot taken from above the scene, usually an exterior shot.

camera angle

The position of the camera in relation to the subject. A shot may be taken from a low-angle, high-angle or eye-level. Different meanings are associated with different camera angles. For e.g. a low angle shot implies power.

close-up (CU)

A shot where the camera, and therefore the audience, is close to the subject e.g. when the head and shoulders of a character fill the screen.

cut

The juxtaposition and joining together of different shots, through editing, in the finished film.

editing

The joining of shots together, by cutting and arranging, to form a sequence. Rapid editing occurs when the sequence has many frames. This can create a sense of panic or urgency.

epic

A heroic tale, usually historical.

establishing shot

The initial shot of a scene, usually from a distance (aerial shot, long shot) showing the viewer where the action is about to occur.

extreme close-up

A shot where the camera is extremely close to the subject, for instance a shot of the eye of an actor only.

extreme long-shot

A shot, usually of an exterior location, taken from a long distance. Usually panoramic.

eye-level shot

Camera viewpoint which represents the view of an observer.

fast motion

A shot in which time is distorted by quickening the pace of the scene.

first person

See point of view shot.

foreground

The part of the shot or scene closest to the viewer, often in front of the action.

foregrounding

Bringing anything to the front, or foreground, of a scene.

genre

Common types or categories of film that are characterised by particular conventions e.g. romantic comedy, action adventure and science fiction are recognisable genres.

insert shot

A shot inserted into a sequence of shots, during editing, to create emphasis. Usually a close-up showing detail.

jump cut

An abrupt but deliberate transition between shots.

long shot (LS)

A shot where the camera is a long way from the subject.

low-angle shot

A shot where the camera is below the subject.

medium shot

A relatively close-up shot of a subject. For instance most of a human figure is evident.

mise-en-scène

The various elements that make up the background of the scene.

montage

A series of shots, rapidly edited together to show the passing of time.

narration

A speaking voice, either from a character on-screen or an off-screen voiceover, that provides commentary on the action or plot.

pan

Also a panning shot, a shot that moves the camera to encompass the full width of a scene.

parallel action

The use of cross-cutting to present multiple stories at the one time.

point of view shot(POV)

A shot that shows the viewer what the character in the film sees.

rapid cutting

A style of editing that juxtaposes short sharp scenes in a sequence.

realism

A genre of film in which authentic locations and details are used to portray reality.

re-establishing shot

Usually follows closer shots, allowing the viewer to recover a sense of the context of the scene.

reverse angle-shot

After one shot the camera turns around to show the same shot from the opposite direction.

scene

An incident in the action, composed of a series of separate but related shots.

score

The background music, separate from the sound track.

screen-play

The written version of the film, including dialogue, description of the action and, sometimes, directions for the camera.

segue

Use of a device to link one scene to another e.g. a voiceover.

sequence

A series of scenes.

shot

A length of film taken without stopping.

slow motion

A shot in which time is distorted by slowing down the action in the scene.

sound

All recorded music, dialogue and background noise. Also the use of silence.

sound track

All of the sound recorded in a film, including the score. (Diegetic sound is the internal sound of the film. Non-diegetic sound is the super-imposed sound placed over and into the film.

symbol

An object or event that represents something else and has meaning beyond the literal.

voiceover

Dialogue spoken off-screen.

wide-shot

A shot taken from a distance, including the entire setting where the action takes place.

zoom

To make the subject appear to approach (zoom-in) or recede (zoom-out) from the camera/viewer.

THE DIRECTOR- STEPHEN DALDRY

The role of the director is to interpret the screenplay in order to create the final product that appears on the screen. Although the director is in charge of the overall vision of the film, he or she will still work in conjunction with a production crew. This process may involve the interpretation of the characters, production design and the composition of the frame.

Billy Elliot (2000) was director Stephen Daldry's first major feature film. Daldry made his own transition from a successful fifteen year career in the theatre. Daldry is the son of singer and bank manager who first developed his talent for the stage as an apprentice to the Italian clown, Elder Molletti and as a member of youth drama group in Taunton England.

After establishing his directorial work by being part of the Crucible Theatre in Sheffield from 1985 to 1988, Daldry travelled to London to direct over 100 plays as part of the fringe theatre, The Gate. Daldry converted this small fringe theatre to suit a more international audience. Daldry began to receive recognition and accolades for his work. The visionary production and deconstructionist staging of J. B Priestly's *An Inspector Calls*, received a Tony Award when the production transferred to Broadway.

Daldry, at the age of 32, was then appointed as Director of the Royal Court where he held the position of Artistic Director from 1992 to 1995. This was a significant transition from a man who was educated at Sheffield University and had a background in radical politics. In the 80s Daldry was a member of Sheffield University Socialist Worker's Party. There, he developed his own political beliefs and knowledge that influenced his productions in the theatre and on film. *An Inspector Calls* can be explored as a critique of Margaret Thatcher's, Britain. Thatcher was the Conservative Prime Minister of Britain from 1979–90.

During this time Daldry was approached by the film production company 'Working Title' to develop a career in film. Daldry first directed the short film *Eight* (1998), followed by *Billy Elliot*, which was originally titled *Dancer*. 'Working Title' is also responsible for other British films such as *Notting Hill* (1999), *Elizabeth* (1998), *Four Weddings and a Funeral* (1994) and the movie, *Love Actually* (2003).

Another aspect of Daldry's personal context which impacted the film *Billy Elliot* was the death of his father from cancer, when Daldry was only fourteen. Daldry worked his own emotions into the film as Billy's mother died when Billy was young.

Daldry's productions also include *The Hours* (2002) staring Nicole Kidman, Meryl Streep and Julian Moore. This is an adaptation of Michael Cunningham's novel which is, itself, a derivative of Virginia Woolf's novel, *Mrs Dalloway*. He also directed *The Reader (2008), Trash (2014),* a film based on a novel and set in Rio and a series for Netflix titled *The Crown (2016-forthcoming). Extremely Loud and Incredibly Close (2011)* was another of his films nominated at the Academy Awards.

BILLY ELLIOT

INSIDE EVERY ONE OF US IS A SPECIAL TALENT WAITING TO COME OUT.

THE TRICK IS FINDING IT.

SCENES

1. Main titles

2. A Disgrace in the Gloves

3. The Ballet Class

4. To Be a Dancer

5. Dad Finds Out

6. Mrs Wilkinson's Offer

7. Private Lessons

8. A Ghost Story

9. Tony's Arrest

10. The Chance to Dance

11. Christmas

12. A Dance of Defiance

13. Dad's Decision

14. The Audition

15. The Interview

16. The Letter

17. Billy's Big Night

18. End Titles

PRODUCTION, CHARACTER AND CAST NAMES

FOR BILLY ELLIOT – UNIVERSAL (2000)
(105 minutes)
Rated M

- Director - Stephen Daldry. Screenplay by Lee Hall. Produced by Greg Brenman and Jon Finn. Natascha Wharton, Charles Brand, Tessa Ross and David M. Thompson all Executive Producers. Brain Tufano, Director of Photography. Maria Djurkovic as Production Designer, John Wilson as Editor, Stewart Meachem as Costume Designer, Peter Darling as Choreographer, and Stephen Warbeck, Composer.

Jamie Bell.............................	Billy Elliot
Gary Lewis.............................	Dad/ Jacky Elliot
Julie Walters.........................	Mrs Wilkinson
Jamie Draven........................	Tony Elliot
Jean Heywood.......................	Grandma
Stuart Wells...........................	Michael Caffrey
Nicola Blackwell....................	Debbie Wilkinson
Mike Elliot.............................	George Watson
Janine Birkett.......................	Billy's Mum
Billy Fane.............................	Mr Braithwaite
Adam Cooper........................	Billy Elliot at age 25
Carol Mc Guigan....................	The Librarian
Joe Renton............................	Gary Poulson
Colin Mac Lachlan..................	Mr Tom Wilkinson
Trevor Fox.............................	P C Jeff Peverly
Charlie Hardwick...................	Sheila Briggs

PLOT OUTLINE

Jacky and Tony are miners who are out on strike

Billy Elliot lives with his father Jacky, brother Tony and grandmother

Billy is unsuccessful at boxing lessons

Billy's interest in ballet develops

Billy is afraid that only "poofs" do ballet

Billy takes part in his first ballet lesson

Debbie persuades Billy that dancers are as fit as athletes

Billy's dad finds out about the lessons

Mrs Wilkinson tells Billy that he is good enough for the Royal Ballet School

Mrs Wilkinson offers Billy private lessons

Tony is arrested by the police, Billy misses out on the Newcastle audition

The Elliot family find out about Billy's dream

Jacky Elliot crosses the picket line for Billy

Billy dances for his father at Christmas in an act of defiance

The audition and interview

Jacky sells his deceased wife's jewellery to pay the fare to London

Billy is accepted into the Royal Ballet School

Billy becomes a successful Ballet Dancer

PLOT SUMMARY AND ANALYSIS

Main Titles

Summary

The movie begins with an unidentified figure placing a record on a turntable. This salient image is centrally positioned in the frame. The song 'Cosmic Dancer' by T-Rex begins to play diegetically as the slow motion shot reveals a young adolescent male jumping on the bed. The boy, the protagonist of the film, *Billy Elliot*, seems to be enjoying the experience. This is evident in the various gestures and facial expressions he is making.

The shot cuts to a long shot of Billy jumping on the bed as the title of the film appears. The scene progresses to Billy who is getting breakfast. The music acts non-diegetically as part of the sound track. His behaviour is typical of a boy his age; catching the toast with his plate and opening the sliding doors with his head. The person for whom he is fixing breakfast has gone. Billy runs out of the house to find his grandmother in a nearby park. Above the park police are getting out of vans and getting their riot gear ready in their daily assignment of controlling the violent striking miners.

The music ends in the next shot when Billy is in bed. Tony, Billy's brother accuses Billy of playing his records.

The shot cuts to the next day. Billy is seated at the piano. Tony and Billy's father Jacky are getting ready to join the picket line. Jacky Elliot disapproves of Billy playing the piano. Billy's response is that "Mum would have let us". The camera tilts up to focus on photographs of Billy's mother. From this scene we gather that Billy's mother has recently passed away.

Analysis

The beginning scene introduces viewers to the Elliot family and provides an orientation. The protagonist, Billy is a typical adolescent boy growing up in a working class family in the North-west of England. His actions show that he likes to have fun and joke around but he is also responsible to his family with a duty to look after his Grandmother who displays features of dementia.

The opening sequence establishes the setting of the film or the specific situation we are to examine. Billy Elliot is a young boy growing up in Everington, County Durham with his father Jacky, older brother Tony and grandmother, during the strike of 1984.

This scene establishes music as an important feature of the film. The music chosen to accompany this scene matches a central theme of the film, which is dance and the freedom of expression it brings. At the beginning of the film, the music belongs to Billy's brother Tony, and is also associated with the piano that Billy's father does not want him to play. A nostalgic sound track is used to allude to the memories of Billy's mother.

Questions

1. Music plays an important role in Billy Elliot. How does music shape our response to the film?

2. The music of T-Rex plays an important role in supporting the narrative. Using the Internet and other resources, research the context of this rock group.

3. Evaluate how Jamie Bell's facial expressions and body language establish Billy's personality.

4. Use the table on the following page to guide your analysis of *Billy Elliot*. Remember that not all of the characters experience transition or change. You can compare the characters that transition with those that do not.

Character	Context	WHY do they move?	WHERE are they going?	HOW is this represented?
BILLY				
JACKY				
TONY				
MRS WILKINSON				
MICHAEL				

A Disgrace in the Gloves

Summary

The scene begins with an establishment shot revealing the violence of the picket line. Tony is in the midst of the action yelling abuse at the police officers. The shot cuts to a long shot of Billy outside the boxing studio talking to his best friend Michael. As they talk, other boys push past Billy to get inside. From their discussion, we find that Billy is not good at boxing. The old gloves he is using which "went out with the ark," belonged to his father.

When Billy enters the boxing club in the next shot, the class has already started. He enters the ring to start sparring with another boy of the same age. As the bell for the beginning of the round sounds, so does the piano for the ballet lesson. The ballet lesson is taking place in the bottom half of the boxing hall as downstairs, where the ballet lessons are usually held, is being used for a soup kitchen for the striking miners.

Instead of boxing properly, Billy begins to respond childishly to the music. It seems as if he does not want to hit his opponent and is using this behaviour to compensate for his lack of focus on boxing. From George Watson, the boxing coach's reaction, we gather that Billy has employed diversionary tactics before when in the ring.

The scene progresses. The boys are sparring in a shot-reverse-shot transition. Jacky Elliot is watching from the sidelines. Jacky yells to Billy to hit the other boy but ironically Billy is distracted and is knocked to the floor by his opponent.

George tells Billy "Jesus Christ Billy Elliot, you're a disgrace to them gloves, your father and the traditions of this boxing hall..."

Analysis

From this scene we gather that boxing is a tradition not only for the males in the Elliot family but for the wider community as well. It is expected that Billy should take this sport seriously. A negative attitude towards dance especially ballet is established in this scene by the dialogue. George Watson tells Billy that it "is man to man combat, not a bloody... dance". A common belief is presented, that to be masculine is to be involved with a 'real' sport such as boxing.

This scene is also building the framework of the complication that will develop for Billy as he makes his transition to become an adult. Billy is part of the world of mining and boxing. It is expected that this is the world in which he will stay.

Questions

1. Compose an Information Report on the 1984 miners' strike.

2. Why are traditions important? Describe some of your family's traditions.

3. Which sports are traditionally masculine and which sports are seen as traditionally geared towards females? Are these gender patterns in sport being challenged nowadays?

The Ballet Class

Summary

Billy is at the punching bag where he is told to remain until he trains properly. He has been given the responsibility to give the keys to Mrs Wilkinson when he has finished. Billy soon loses interest in the bag. The shot cuts to a point-of-view shot from Billy observing Mrs Wilkinson and the piano accompanist, Mr Braithwaite. This technique enables the responder to view the events from Billy's position, which creates identification with the protagonist. Mrs Wilkinson is smoking and is not really concentrating on the girls undertaking the lesson.

As the shot cuts back to Billy, he begins to move in time to the music and the swaying of the punching bag. It seems as if Mrs Wilkinson's instructions for her lesson are also meant for him. Billy begins to punch the bag rhythmically to the music and the count that Mrs Wilkinson is providing. As Billy's interest in the lesson becomes obvious, a flute sounds in the non-diegetic soundtrack.

In the next shot Billy seems to be observing the lesson. Girls dance in the foreground. Billy's reflection is seen in the frame. As the girls move into the centre, a medium long shot of Billy's refection is trapped with the frame of the mirror and the real Billy is seen trying to give the smoking Mrs Wilkinson the keys. Billy is asked by Debbie, the daughter of Mrs Wilkinson, to join the lesson but he responds negatively. Amusingly, the next shot is a tracking shot of the girls practising their steps and Billy is in the midst of them, copying the move. The close up of the ballet slippers is juxtaposed with Billy's blue boxing boots.

In the centre of the room at the barre, the dancers are now performing side leg raises. Mrs Wilkinson begins to walk alongside the dancers and tells them to hold the movement. She notices Billy's natural talent for ballet and his foot's high arch when pointed. Billy displays "a nice straight leg with good arch." The class is dismissed.

On the way home Mrs Wilkinson and Debbie pull up next to Billy to ask him for the 50p for that lesson. Billy's response is that he does not owe her anything. Mrs Wilkinson asks Billy whether he enjoyed it but he does not answer. They drive off leaving Billy in the middle of the road. 'Top Hat White Tie and Tails' performed by Fred Astaire begins to play in the background acting as a segue to the next shot which is the source of sound track; an excerpt from the movie *Top Hat (1935)*.

The scene moves in another direction with a dissolve to an extreme long shot of Billy and his grandmother walking across the horizon. The setting of the green grass of the cemetery is juxtaposed with the harsh industrial buildings and factories in the background. Billy's grandmother is telling Billy about the time when she was young and his mother was a girl. They would go to the Palace Picture house to watch movies and dance in front of the theatre like "lunatics". Fred Astaire was his mother's favourite. A medium long shot of Billy's grandmother framed by two chimneys precedes her statement that she could have been a professional dancer.

At his mother's grave, Billy throws away empty alcohol cans and attempts to clean the graffiti off the headstone. He even trims the grass with scissors that he has brought with him. The piano refrain which is linked with Billy's mother, is heard in the sound track. According to the tombstone, Billy's mother died less than a year earlier at age 38. The grandmother is at the wrong grave. The scene ends at night when Billy is about to go to sleep. He asks his brother if he ever thinks about death. Billy is met with a curt reply.

Analysis

The scene presents Billy's growing attraction to dance and the natural gift he has for ballet. At this stage in the film, Billy is confused about what he should do, boxing or ballet? He enjoyed the class but he is also aware of what his family would think. It is as if he is split in two. The framing used within the scene represents this. The reflection of Billy trapped by the frame of the mirror is symbolic of his growing up and developing interest in dance. Billy is confined to the expectations of his social and cultural context. Billy wants to take his first transitional steps into a different personal and social context but is confused about how he should make those steps. He is portrayed as a thoughtful, sensitive, creative boy who seeks change in order to be true to himself, his talents and dreams.

Questions

1. How do we know Billy enjoyed the lesson?

2. Describe how the features of shot sizes and camera angles make Billy stand out in the lesson?

3. List your first impressions of Mrs Wilkinson.

4. Fred Astaire is a popular dance figure of the classic films of Hollywood. He has been hailed as the greatest dancer to ever have graced the silver screen. Astaire had genius, was grace personified and was regarded by many as a naturally gifted dancer.

5. Explain the symbolism of the excerpt from *Top Hat*.

6. Why is it important to know that Billy's grandmother could have been a professional dancer?

To Be a Dancer

Summary

The scene begins with a tracking shot of Debbie and Billy walking down the street in their school uniforms. Debbie is dragging a stick along the brick wall and the prominently displayed 'Strike Now' posters that are plastered over them. Sirens can be heard in the distance. The two walk past riot police and Debbie continues to drag her stick across their shields as if it was a normal everyday occurrence or as if the police were not there. Debbie is encouraging Billy to continue with the ballet lessons. She is trying to convince Billy that all male ballet dancers are not "poofs" but are, in fact, fit athletes.

Billy and Debbie pause in a long shot in front of a billboard. Half of the advertisement is not there. Ironically, the image is of a Servis washing machine with a masculine figure positioned as if he is coming out of the front loading washing machine. The text on the advertisement reads, "your ever- faithful washday slave" suggesting that the man as well as the washing machine are slaves.

The scene changes quickly to Billy at the piano, then Billy in the change rooms as he is sneaking into the ballet lesson. In the lesson he finds himself lost in the dance moves and is told to follow the others. At the end of the lesson Mrs Wilkinson asks Billy if he will continue to attend the class next week. Billy's response is that he feels like a "right sissy". Mrs Wilkinson replies, "then don't act like one."

The next shot is of Billy at home hiding his ballet shoes underneath his mattress. He is almost caught by his father who reinforces the belief that boxing is a masculine tradition.

The song 'Get It On' by T-Rex plays on the sound track as the scene moves to Billy at school. In a Physical Education class with Michael, they are undertaking a cross-country run. Michael takes Billy on a short cut where he then asks Billy about the ballet lessons. Michael asks Billy if he gets to wear a tutu. Billy's response is that tutus are for girls and that he just wears his shorts. Michael suggests that Billy would look "wicked" in a tutu. They continue to run.

The next shot is of Billy going to the Durham County mobile library. Billy is looking at a book on ballet but is told he can't borrow it on a junior ticket. While the librarian is distracted, Billy steals the book. Using the book Billy practices the first arabesque in the bathroom. This is contrasted with the parallel scenes of Billy performing the same movement in his bedroom and the lessons. Billy finally has success as a dancer and he dances all the way home.

Analysis

This scene explores various issues relating to gender. Gender is more that just physical differences between male and female. A person's gender is constructed by society's expectations about how to act as a female and a male. Billy assumes that all ballet dancers are homosexuals which is a belief shared by his family and the wider community. Debbie tells him otherwise, assuring him that real men do dance and are, in fact, as fit as athletes.

Throughout this scene Billy contemplates whether he should move or transition into the world of dance. He is aware of his father's negative reaction.

The advertisement in the background suggests that females and males are not limited to stereotypical gender roles. Males can do the washing just as well as they can dance. When Billy is feeling silly about his performance as a dancer, he is told not to act like a sissy. Gender is an act or, in other words is a performance. In fact, it is Michael who is experimenting with his sexual identity.

Questions

1. How does this scene present the idea that the strike has become a normal part of life for the community? For example, consider the shot where Debbie and Billy walk past the riot police without noticing them.

2. Define gender.

3. What part of the dialogue supports the concept that gender is more than the sexual difference between being male and female?

4. What is the relationship between the various posters and billboards that are presented as part of the mise-en-scène and the plot?

Dad Finds Out

Summary

The scene commences back at the picket line. The boxing trainer George Watson, is telling Jacky Elliot that he hasn't seen Billy or Jacky for months. As the bus crosses the picket line the violence and anger of the striking miners erupts. The aerial shot of the picket line is contrasted with the power and grace of Billy's dance moves. Now it seems that Mrs Wilkinson's instructions are also commenting on Jacky on the picket line.

When Billy is sneaking out to a lesson, a news radio broadcast of Margaret Thatcher is playing in the background. The radio announcer says, "In a speech to Tory M.P's yesterday, Prime Minister Margaret Thatcher referred to members of the striking National Union of Mine Workers as the 'enemy within'." Billy walks through a number of police to get to the lesson. In the middle of the lesson, Jacky arrives and orders Billy out.

At home, Jacky argues with Billy over ballet. Billy sees that there is nothing wrong with ballet but his father's response is that ballet is for girls "not for lads Billy, lads to football, boxing or wrestling. Not frigging ballet." The shot changes to a close up of Billy's face as he responds to his father's words. Father and son end in a scuffle where Billy leaves the house in anger and frustration. The 'Children of the Revolution' sound track by T-Rex is heard. Billy runs away and takes his anger out on another "Strike Now' poster.

The scene cuts to Billy now in school uniform walking through a middle class suburb which contrasts with his own. The houses are not crammed together and have lawns with cars parked out the front. Billy arrives at the Wilkinson's where he informs Mrs Wilkinson that his father won't allow him to attend class anymore. Billy stays for tea, during which time we find out that the Wilkinsons have problems of their own. Mr Wilkinson is also out of work. From his middle class viewpoint, we are also provided with more information about the context of the miners' strike.

Throughout this scene we also observe Billy and Debbie's relationship develop. Debbie seems to know more about her parents than they realise.

Analysis

The scene establishes the belief systems held by Jacky Elliot and the wider working class Durham community. Boys do not do ballet; rather they follow sports that are more 'masculine'. Not only is Billy restricted by the gender expectations of his society; he is also constricted by the impoverished socioeconomic situation his family faces due to the miner's strike. The scene also establishes Jacky's character. He struggles to give Billy the 50p each week, let alone provide food for his family. Focus on how the film represents Billy and how his family reacts to changes and transitions which are seen as challenging the status quo.

Jacky Elliot's discovery regarding his son's dancing places another restriction on Billy's transition to self-fulfilled dancer. The reference to the striking miners as the "enemy within" may also be relevant to Jacky's function in becoming an obstacle in Billy's desire to lead his own life.

Questions

1. Who is Margaret Thatcher? Composes a feature article that explores Margaret Thatcher's England and her political beliefs.

2. What is the function of the radio excerpt that refers to Margaret Thatcher?

3. Evaluate the similarities and differences between the action on the picket line and the ballet lesson.

4. Why is the framing of Mrs Wilkinson's street different to that of Billy's neighbourhood?

Mrs Wilkinson's Offer

Summary

As Mrs Wilkinson is dropping Billy off at the corner, she tells Billy of her intention to try him out for the Royal Ballet School. Billy believes that he is not good enough. Mrs Wilkinson reassures him by telling him that they are interested in potential "...it is how you move and express yourself that is important." Mrs Wilkinson offers to tutor him privately, without payment, and without his father knowing.

The scene shifts as Billy arrives at Michael's house. Michael is dressing up in his sister's clothes and is putting make up on. When Billy asks him if he'll get into trouble if anyone sees him, Michael says they won't. During their conversation we realise that Michael's father also dresses in female clothes. Michael puts lipstick on Billy. Billy asks Michael the question, "Do you think being a ballet dancer would be better than being a man?"

Billy talks to Michael about the idea of ballet school and the consequences of telling his father.

Analysis

From this scene we see the relationship between Billy and Mrs Wilkinson develop. They talk and argue with each other as equals, rather than as teacher and student. Not only is Billy expressing doubt in his own ability but also he is also afraid of the consequences if his father finds out about the private lessons.

The concept of gender is further explored at Michael's house. Billy is finding freedom and self- expression through dance but it is Michael who is experimenting with his sexuality by dressing in female clothes.

Private Lessons

Summary

This scene shows Billy's first private lesson. He has brought special things with him as inspiration for a dance he would use for his audition. Billy's shadow first enters the frame, followed by a long shot of the real Billy walking into the boxing hall. The scene cuts to another long shot but this time it is from Billy's point-of-view. The natural lighting highlights Mrs Wilkinson in the background of the frame.

One of the items Billy has brought with him is a letter written to him by his mother. Mrs Wilkinson begins to read the letter out aloud but Billy knows the letter off by heart and finishes it for her. An important piece of advice given to Billy is to "always be yourself". The piano sound track enhances the nostalgic atmosphere.

The following dance sequence is to the 'I Love to Boogie' tape, which is also performed by T-Rex. The shots of Mrs Wilkinson and Billy dancing to the energetic and upbeat music are contrasted with the parallel shots of this same music in the Elliot home. Billy's brother Tony is in his bedroom using a carpet cleaner as a guitar, their grandmother is practising a ballet position and Jacky is having a bath.

The scene moves to early morning where Tony is sneaking out of the house. He wants to fight against the situation of hopelessness caused by the miners' strike. Jacky is awake and anticipating Tony's actions. In an intensely dramatic episode, Jacky punches Tony in the face after his son yells at him, saying that his father has not been a real man since the death of his mother. The tension is highlighted during a slow motion shot of Billy yelling, "Stop it," in reaction to the violent outburst.

The scene moves to Billy in the middle of another private lesson. The lesson is not going well. Billy is not landing a pirouette en dehors. Mrs Wilkinson's reaction is to tell Billy to concentrate but Billy just runs away to find solace in the change rooms. Mrs Wilkinson and Billy have a heated exchange of their own. The argument ends in a medium close up of Mrs Wilkinson comforting Billy. The next shot is a long shot of Billy practising the same pirouette movement but this time it is represented by the reflection in a mirror.

Analysis

From this moving scene we learn of the relationship Billy had with his mother and the nurturing care he is missing. It seems that Mrs Wilkinson is taking on the role of nurturer. Not only does Billy take his anguish out on her but he also turns to her for comfort.

Tony's character also develops in this scene. He is not one who will let the situation of the strike pass him by. He wants to be a man of action, even if these actions may be illegal.

Questions

1. Explain the symbolism of Billy's shadow entering the frame.

2. How does the use of lighting shape our feelings in this scene?

3. From the information presented in this scene, describe the relationship that Billy had with his mother.

4. Discuss the symbolism of the special things Billy has brought with him.

A Ghost Story

Summary

This scene commences with an establishing shot of Billy and Mrs Wilkinson driving. Billy wants to play a tape and the music of *Swan Lake* begins to play in the background. On the ferry Mrs Wilkinson recounts the story of the famous ballet *Swan Lake*. It is the story of a beautiful, young woman who is transformed into a swan. Only a prince can allow her to become a woman once more but he leaves her for another woman, resulting in the death of the beautiful young girl. Mrs Wilkinson said that this is only a ghost story. The setting of the mechanical docklands is juxtaposed with the beautiful sound track.

Billy is now in the kitchen at night. The camera pans to reveal the ghost of Billy's mother who tells him to not drink out of the bottle and to put the milk back into the fridge.

Billy is now rehearsing at the barre with Mrs Wilkinson. A tracking shot frames 360° of the graceful ballet movements. The scene changes to Billy who is now talking with Debbie. Debbie also does not want him to leave.

Analysis

The scene presents the idea of ghosts. A comparison can be made between the beautiful young girl of *Swan Lake* and Billy's mother who also died prematurely. Billy is also making progress in developing his ballet skills. The movements in this scene are graceful like a swan.

Questions

1. What is the function of ghosts in this scene?

Tony's Arrest

Summary

The scene begins with a long shot of the riot police advancing on the strikers. Tony escapes into a house and the police give chase. The action of the scene is supported by the music of

The Clash performing 'London Calling' in the sound track. The camera follows Tony in a jerking fashion as he runs through the houses. Tony steals sips of tea and spits on a police car. Billy is watching the event from the fence of a nearby house. Tony is caught as he becomes tangled in washing drying on a clothesline.

Billy calls Mrs Wilkinson to say that he has a problem with the audition due to take place the next day. Debbie answers and hangs up on him. The scene concludes with Mrs Wilkinson arriving the next day at the Elliot's house.

Analysis

This short scene confirms the feeling of inequality between the miners and the government who are represented by the faceless police. The miners have little chance against the sheer number of police.

The community show their support for Tony as he runs through the various homes. The humour of this scene is short-lived as the prevailing sense of injustice, where the police set upon the unarmed Tony, overrides.

Questions

1. How do framing and editing techniques enhance the tension as Tony runs from the law?

The Chance to Dance

Summary

Tony, Jacky and Billy arrive home from the police station to find the waiting Mrs Wilkinson. Mrs Wilkinson tells the Elliot family about Billy's audition for the Royal Ballet School. Tony is the most vocal in this scene expressing disapproval of his brother's dancing. Billy expresses his desire to be a dancer. Tony forces Billy to dance on the kitchen table to prove himself. The shot transfers to Billy's point-of-view as the audience watches the argument between his family and Mrs Wilkinson. The shot is intercut with a quick flash of Billy dancing outside, only to return to the argument between Tony and Mrs Wilkinson which is occurring inside. The argument is drowned out by the sound track, 'Town Called Malice' that was written by Paul Weller and performed by The Jam. When Mrs Wilkinson leaves, the scene moves to Billy who is in the back yard.

The scene transforms into a dance sequence where Billy is displaying his frustration and anger. There is a long shot of Billy dancing along a brick wall in their backyard. He runs his hands across the rough brick surface. Billy then kicks down the blue toilet door and continues to run through the back streets of his neighbourhood, tapping all the way down the empty street and running into a rusty, cast iron wall. Michael calls Billy but the change in the setting to a snow filled street indicates that some time has passed.

Analysis

The scene explores the motif of Billy dancing and the wall, a symbol of the obstacles in his journey of transition. The wall represents the barriers he is facing; those of gender expectations, family position and the financial situation the strike has put his family in. There is no break in the wall symbolising that he is trapped but there is hope. Billy kicks the blue toilet door down suggesting that these barriers can be transcended. He wants to kick the wall down but it is beyond his control as an adolescent. The framing of this dance sequence not only allows Billy to display the stylised movements of his whole body but it also enhances the only feeling of freedom he has. Dancing affords Billy the ability to transcend and transition from an impoverished gender based society to one offering greater freedom. It is not until Billy's family interferes in his decision to audition for the Royal Ballet School that he verbalises that this is what he wants to do for the rest of his life.

Questions

1. Explain the impact of the point-of-view shot taken from Billy's perspective, on the viewer.

2. How do the camera and dialogue combine to create the status of the characters? Refer to camera angles, shot size and dialogue.

3. Why do you think Jacky Elliot remains relatively silent during this scene?

4. How does the scene represent the development in Billy's relationship with his environment?

Christmas

Summary

The scene begins with the miners rallying together. George, the boxing coach, is leading a chorus of "Here we go." The scene changes to show Jacky cutting up the piano for firewood. The sound of the axe hitting the piano resonates to indicate the emotional impact that this act has on the family. Jacky begins to sob while Billy and the Grandmother are eating their Christmas meal.

The shot transitions to change to Billy and Michael who are making snowmen. During their discussion Billy tells Michael, "Just because I like ballet doesn't mean that I am a poof you know." Michael confides his sexuality to Billy.

Analysis

From this scene, we can tell that the family's financial situation has worsened. They do not have enough money to afford proper heating materials. Ironically, most of the houses would have been heated by burning coal. The destruction of the piano marks one less source of creativity within the Elliot household.

The theme of gender is also present in this scene. Billy confirms his heterosexual status while Michael voices his homosexuality, alluded to in previous scenes. Billy is accepting of his best friend's transition into the world of his choice. This promotes the value of tolerance which is imbedded in the film's ideology. A message is conveyed, we should be more accepting about how others want to lead their lives.

Questions
1. Why is it important to know that Billy is not gay?

A Dance of Defiance

Summary

Billy and Michael sneak into the boxing club. Billy gives Michael a tutu and teaches him some ballet positions. The drunken George observes the boys and runs to get Jacky to come and see for himself. In an act of defiance, Billy dances the audition piece for his father to show him what he can do but Jacky just walks out. Michael claps uncomfortably. The strong rhythm and dynamics of the music match Billy's emotions and reveal the pride he has in his love for dance.

Analysis

The dance of defiance is a pivotal scene in Billy's transition. It is in this scene that Jacky actually gets to see him dance and realises his son has talent as a dancer. Billy is also not afraid to stand up to his father by spontaneously dancing for him. It is through this confrontation over dance that Billy and his father grow closer, despite their differences.

This is a major step in Billy's transition. He is doing what he loves, despite what others think and what may follow.

Questions
1. Explore how Billy's dance movements are symbolic of transition.

Dad's Decision

Summary

It is still Christmas, Jacky Elliot confronts Mrs Wilkinson about how much the audition will cost. He thanks her for all she has done for his son but tells her that because Billy is his son, he now needs to take responsibility.

The first decision Jacky Elliot makes is to go back to work and cross the picket like so that he can afford to take Billy to London. As the bus crosses the picket line, Tony sees his father on the bus. The music sound track supports the emotions of the scene when Tony confronts his father. Jacky has gone against everything that the family has gone through and fought for as a result of the strike. Jacky breaks down and does not go though with going back to work. He then makes his next difficult decision, which is to pawn his wife's jewellery to pay for the trip to London. While Billy and Jacky are on the bus to the audition, we discover that this is also Jacky's first time to London.

Analysis

During this scene Jacky swallows his pride to give his son a chance. He has made his own transition to overcome his own misconceptions and established principles. It proves that despite his harsh exterior, Jacky does love his son and only wants the best for him. Jacky has also been confined by societal expectations. He has not had the opportunity to step out of his own mining community.

Questions

1. Why doesn't Jacky Elliot accept Mrs Wilkinson's offer to pay for the trip to London?

2. Who has the status in the conversation that Jacky has with Mrs Wilkinson? How can we tell this from the film techniques used by the composer?

The Audition

Summary

Jacky and Billy arrive in London. As they enter the Royal Ballet School the aerial long shot of Billy suggests that Billy is engulfed and overwhelmed by the situation. While waiting for the audition to begin, Billy seems to be overcome by nerves but Jacky reassures him and forces him back into the room. In the change rooms other boys are also preparing for their auditions. We overhear a young blonde boy's conversation with another boy who is auditioning. He says that this is his second audition. He then talks to Billy and asks him where he is from. Billy replies Durham County. The boy asks him about an amazing cathedral that is in that location but Billy has not seen it.

During the audition piece the medium long shots of the panel show a lack of emotional response. When the audition ends, Billy storms back into the change rooms despondent. Another young boy goes to Billy and attempts to comfort him. Billy is not used to the physical contact or sensitivity from an outsider let alone another male and reacts to the situation by punching the other boy and calling him a "bent bastard'.

Analysis

This is Billy's first time in the big city but from his conversation with the other boys who are auditioning we realise that Billy has not seen the sights of his own County. Durham County is in fact the site of England's finest Norman cathedral. Work on the cathedral began in 1093 and it is considered to be one of the finest architectural achievements in the country. This information highlights how significant the journey to London really was. On the other hand, Billy is faced with unfamiliar responses so he falls back onto the behaviour he has learnt from his father and brother. This seems unusual for Billy given his friendship with Michael. This is Billy's big day. It is everything that he has been working towards but it seems he is not able to deal with the pressure of his first and most important audition.

Questions

1. How do the film techniques portray Billy's emotions in this scene?

2. What would you say to defend Billy's actions in the locker room?

The Interview

Summary

The scene begins with a long shot of Billy and Jacky sitting in the audition space. Again, the framing suggests that the Elliots are overcome by the situation. The head member of the audition panel tells Billy and Jacky that Billy's actions may have negative consequences and that type of behaviour is not tolerated at their establishment. He proceeds to ask questions regarding Billy's interest in ballet. Billy's answers are not developed or substantial. The member of the audition panel asks Jacky whether he is a fan of the ballet and proceeds to explain the importance of having the total support of the family. This is the first time that we see Jacky verbalise the support he has for his son. Jacky is also trying to make up for Billy's lack of answers to the interview questions.

The members of the audition panel then give the Elliots the opportunity to ask them any questions. As there aren't any, Jacky and Billy stand to leave. At that moment another female panel member asks Billy just one last question. She asks him what it feel like when he is dancing. Billy's reply is, "Dunno, sort of feels good. Sort of safe … but when I get going…I forget everything… um I sort of disappear, sort of disappear, I can feel a change in my whole body, just this fire in my body just there; like a bird, like electricity, yeah, like electricity." Billy verbalises in this quotation the transition he undergoes when dancing.

The interview ends with the head panel member wishing the Elliots well with the strike.

Analysis

The purpose of the interview is for the audition panel to gain an holistic impression of Billy and his family. Billy's answer to the final question is most interesting. His response describes the sensation of transformation through dance. By disappearing he is not only affected by the world and by saying that he feels a change, like a bird, expresses the freedom and liberation that dancing gives him. Fire and electricity connote the energy and power that he also feels while dancing.

The audition panel are also familiar with Billy's situational context and are aware of the effects of the miners' strike, which reinforces the fact that it is a national issue.

Questions

1. How do the film techniques used during the dance sequences portray Billy feeling like electricity?

2. Have a go at storyboarding one of the dance sequences. A storyboard is a way of mapping out what happens in a scene frame by frame. Be careful to pay attention to the framing and camera angles that are used to express the excitement of Billy dancing.

3. Describe the gestures and facial expressions that Jacky and Billy make that suggest that this London world of ballet auditions is alien to them.

The Letter

Summary

Jacky, Billy and Nan are sitting, waiting. Nan tells Billy that he should get himself a trade, something useful. She reminds the family that she could have been a professional dancer. The shot changes to Billy at school, in class with Michael. The post arrives in another shot with the letter. Billy arrives home with his family waiting for him at the kitchen table. Billy goes onto the next room to read the letter. The medium close up of Billy's reaction to reading the letter does not confirm its contents one way or another. As his family join him, the crying Billy announces to them that he has been accepted.

Jacky excitedly runs up the street. It is the same street that Billy had previously danced down. Jacky goes to tell his fellow miners the good news. He is told that the workers' union caved in, the strike is over and the miners are now going back to work. The shot cuts to Billy and Jacky at the cemetery. They are happy, laughing and joking around.

Billy goes to the hall where Mrs Wilkinson is giving a lesson to tell her the news but she already knows. She asks him, "Does this mean you will go out and find life and all those other things?" She wishes Billy well and continues with the lesson.

Billy says goodbye to Michael. While Billy is on the bus, Tony says that he will miss him but Billy cannot hear him. The scene shifts to Tony and Jacky who are back at work, Mrs Wilkinson who is alone in the boxing club then to Billy finally leaving on the bus. The scene concludes with a dissolve.

Analysis

Billy has gained entry into the exclusive Royal Ballet School. It seems as if the hard work has paid off to allow Billy to make his transition and live happily ever after. Billy is, in fact, moving on. He is finding life, his life. Not only is his family supportive of his decision to dance and are happier but the greater community was also looking out for the news of Billy receiving the letter. Jacky is laughing with his youngest son and Tony even expresses that he will miss his younger brother.

Although the news of Billy's success is positive, it is met with the disappointing news that the strike has been unsuccessful. Life returns to normal for Jacky and Tony as they resume working life down the pits. They may have grown emotionally in developing acceptance and support of Billy dancing but their lives have not really changed.

Mrs Wilkinson's life also returns to normal. She remains in a loveless marriage, teaching the same ballet class. She may not have had the talent to be a professional dancer herself but she has been able to use her skills to help Billy. Billy has made her life more meaningful. She has found hope in his potential but we do not know if she will make a greater effort in teaching her regular ballet classes. The life that Billy will go out and find is the life she missed out on.

Questions

1. Why do you think Billy waited to tell Mrs Wilkinson that he got accepted into the Royal Ballet School?

Billy's Big Night

Summary

The scene commences with the continuation of the dissolve of Jacky and Tony on an underground train. They alight at Haymarket, arriving to watch Billy's performance at the Theatre Royale. Fourteen years have passed and Billy is now a professional dancer. Jacky and Tony are late and are hurriedly seated next to a grown up Michael and his partner. The performance begins, starting with the music of *Swan Lake*. Jacky is overcome with emotion.

The shot changes to a medium close up of the back of the adult Billy about to get ready for his entrance. The lighting is from above and Billy is surrounded by a surreal glow. The music grows with the anticipation and Billy begins to warm up. The frame is a close up of Billy when he is told that his family is there. We assume from the music and costume that Billy has a main role in the performance. The other chorus dancers are waiting for Billy to enter. The moment we all have been waiting for begins as Billy leaps into the air triumphantly. The scene ends with Billy frozen in position.

Analysis

The scene marks the culmination of Billy's efforts to make a transition. He has grown up. He has achieved success. He defied gender and class stereotypes to follow his talents and passion. *Swan Lake* is no longer a ghost story but is in fact a triumphant reality. The response he made at the audition interview has come true. Not only is the mise-en-scène of his costume a bird, but it also seems that he is literally filled with fire. Electricity filled the air in anticipation of Billy's entrance.

Michael has also grown up and is being true to himself. He has moved into his world despite what others may think of him.

Questions

1. What is Billy's final leap in the air symbolic of?

2. What is the function of the ballet *Swan Lake*?

3. Evaluate the film techniques that represent Billy's success.

End Titles

Summary

The film ends where it began with Billy jumping on his bed to the song that says, "If I believe that I can do anything". In the background is the adult Billy performing the pirouettes that he found difficult but now completes perfectly.

Analysis

The final sequence reinforces the belief that if you put your mind to it, you can do anything. The film leaves us with images of the young Billy Elliot to remind us where he came from.

SETTING

The setting for *Billy Elliot* is the fictional Everington, a coastal pit village of County Durham, situated in Northern England. Everington is in fact the real mining village Easington. The film is set in 1984 amidst the context of Britain's worst industrial dispute in the country's post war history. Easington was ironically one of the biggest coal producing town in Europe before the strike. Many of the extras at the picket lines were real miners who actually went out on strike in 1984.

The year long miners' strike had a tremendous impact on the Thatcher government and on the economy. The conservative Thatcher government was unwilling to support what it saw as a failing industry for the long term. Tens of thousands of miners went on strike following an announcement that the "uneconomic" pits would have to close, putting 20 000 miners out of work.

The striking action was sidelined by the numerous violent confrontations at the picket lines and the hardships that were evident in the mining communities. More than thirty years on, the impact of the strike is remembered. There are now few deep pits in the United Kingdom still producing coal. In the end the biggest losers were the ordinary miners.

The film examines the relationships of the coal mining family struggling to come to terms with the impact of the strike. The film begins during the early stages of the strike and concludes a year later, when the strike is over. The threat of the strike produced a community that was tightly knit but the end of mining would also result in the end of community.

Billy came from a family with a strong mining and boxing tradition. It was expected that Billy would also become a miner and a boxer just like his father and his father's father. The miner's conflict is reflected in the conflicts in the smaller world of the Elliot household. The working context and the domestic setting faced transition brought about by changed conditions and changing views.

Billy faced his own struggle. His mother had recently passed away leaving him in a male dominated household. Additionally, Billy attempted to discover a means of expressing himself, which he eventually did, through dance. The Elliot family was in crisis; the whole family was confused due to changed circumstances and transitions in many areas of life. The father is unsure of the outcome of the strike, Tony is seems, was certain of absolute victory. Personal relationships, working conditions, family finances, traditions and values and gender roles were all challenged in this film. Transitions or changes to relationships and personal journeys arise due to these factors either singularly or in combination.

The mise-en-scène of the setting reflects the sense of Billy being closed in by his family's situation and the negative impact the strike has on the community. The Elliot household is in a working class community. The houses are all crammed together with little or no greenery. The washing is hung communally, and the toilets are outside. The tight framing enhances the notion that Billy is trapped by his context.

In comparison, the area where the Wilkinsons live is middle class. The mise-en-scène shots reveal greater affluence. Families have cars which are parked outside on lawns and the houses are not fenced in. The Director of Photography, Brian Tofano collaborated with Stephen Daldry to frame "the mining village in a claustrophobic way to reflect the tight knit community. The buildings were a part of the narrative, so we framed them tight and have them spilling outside of the framework.[1]"

1   www.billyelliot.com

CHARACTER ANALYSIS

Billy Elliot

At eleven years of age, Billy is the youngest member of the Elliot household. He is coming to terms with life and with the expectations of manhood. He has been forced to grow up quickly due to the death of his mother and the impoverished economic situation of his family, due to the miner's strike. Billy is a mature person who also has the responsibility of looking after his grandmother. Billy is not only at odds with his family over his desire to become a dancer but is also pitted against the community and the larger, hostile world. Billy goes through tough times but he embraces these experiences to make himself stronger.

Billy turns to dance as a means of artistic expression but it becomes more than that. Dance is also a means of liberation and freedom for Billy. Billy has a spark of something special. Not only is dance a natural gift but he also has the determination to make his dream a reality. This determination also makes his character all the more likeable.

The costumes Billy wears reflect his status in the community. Apart from his school uniform, Billy wears the typical dress of an adolescent growing up in Northern England. When he is not wearing the singlets and shorts he dances in, Billy is seen in worn and faded denim jeans and jacket. Jamie Bell, who has been dancing since he was six years old, performs as Billy Elliot. This is an excellent feat for a first time actor who was cast from thousands of boys who tried out for the role.

What is more interesting are the many characteristics that both Billy and Jamie Bell share. Not only do they have the common gift for dance but are separately pushed to reach their full potential. Jamie was also confronted with the belief that dance is not for boys; it is more for girls. Jamie Bell even came from Billington, a village that is a dozen miles south to where the film is set. This meant that Jamie Bell would speak in the same register as a young boy from Durham County.

Jamie Bell uses gestures and facial expressions to convey Billy's emotions. The facial expressions range from joy and excitement in the opening titles when Billy is jumping to one of his favourite rock songs, to the disappointment and frustration felt after his audition.

Mrs Wilkinson

Mrs Wilkinson is rarely seen without a cigarette in hand while she barks out instructions to her class. She has a daughter who is the same age as Billy but who, unlike Billy, is trapped within a middle class world. Mrs Wilkinson is in a loveless marriage where her husband, who has cheated on her, has been made redundant and now spends most of his time drinking. The function of Mrs Wilkinson's character is important as is she instrumental in facilitating Billy's transition.

Billy's relationship with his dance teacher is a key element in the film. It is Mrs Wilkinson who dares Billy to wear the ballet slippers in the first place and it is she who recognises his talent. She seems to become obsessed with the possibility that Billy progress to the Royal Ballet School. It is obvious from Billy's visit to the Wilkinson household that Billy has been the topic of conversation.

Mrs Wilkinson does not treat Billy like a child; rather they bicker and argue as equals. She takes on a nurturing role as she helps him to fulfil his dream to become a dancer. Mrs Wilkinson may have developed personally in her support for Billy but at the end of the film her circumstances have not changed. She does not go to see Billy's first major performance and her family situation is still the same as she continues to teach ballet to have a sense of fulfilment. She is pivotal to Billy's personal and social transition but she undergoes little change herself.

Mrs Wilkinson does not look like the stereotypical ballet teacher. Her hair and clothes are messy, she chain smokes and she barks out the instructions to her students.

Jacky Elliot

Jacky is the strong patriarch of the family who holds onto traditional masculine values. Although he often turns to violence to solve problems, we should not forget that Jacky has also experienced horrendous changes with the recent death of his wife and the emasculating lack of employment. His world is changing around him but he does not have the emotional capacity to deal with it.

Jacky is too caught up in his own world to realise that his son is sneaking out of the house to go to ballet lessons. He is told by George, the boxing coach, that his son is no longer turning up to boxing. He is hurt when he sees that his son is not going to be a boxer or a football player. Jacky becomes part of Billy's world once he realises his youngest son's talent. Jacky then takes on the responsibility to make Billy's dreams come true, whether it be the sacrifice of pride in crossing the picket line or selling his wife's jewellery. It is on the night of Billy's performance that we see Jacky Elliot stepping out into his familiar context, emotionally and physically.

Gary Lewis has been well cast to play the father who is coming to terms with his emotions. His body language portrays his stubborn nature but this is juxtaposed with the heart-felt emotion of chopping up his wife's piano for firewood at Christmas.

Tony Elliot

It is easy to forget Tony is facing the same hardship as the rest of the family, regarding the loss of his mother and employment. Tony is a loud obnoxious character who selfishly verbalises his opposition to Billy dancing. He appears to be selfish and care only about his world which revolves around the action of the picket line. While confronting a scab miner in the supermarket he yells, "You never cross a picket line...we're all fucked if you forget that."

Tony has confidence in a positive outcome for the strike and is not afraid to take the situation into his own hands, even if it puts him in trouble with the law.

Tony then sees the sacrifice his father made when he crossed the picket line and supported Billy's dancing. We also see another aspect of his character in this scene when he breaks down while comforting his father. It is at this moment we see Tony moving away from the world of the picket line, back to the family and role of sympathetic son.

Michael Caffrey

Michael is Billy's best friend and his character functions to contrast with the gender implications of Billy Elliot's character. Michael's homosexuality reinforces Billy's heterosexuality. Michael is not afraid of what others think of him, whether it is refusing to go to boxing with the rest of the lads or putting on make up and dresses at home. Michael has made his own transition which is evident at his appearance at Billy's big night, the performance that Michael would not miss for the world.

Michael develops a means of self-expression. The composer uses dialogue and mise-en-scène to reveal Michael's transition. Michael is from the same world as Billy. He lives in the same tight knit community with closed in housing and, for many scenes, wears a costume similar to Billy's.

THEMES

- Dance and Music
- Growing Up
- Gender Identity

Dance and Music

Dance is a theme within the film. Not only is it a means of self expression for Billy but it also functions as his means of liberation. The theme of dance was so important that the film was originally called *Dancer*. The theme is established early in the film through the song 'Cosmic Dancer' played as part of the sound track in the main titles.

Dance allows Billy to make his transition; to grow beyond the limitations of his family and community. To be a professional dancer is Billy's dream and the message of the film is to follow your dreams. His dream is met with opposition through society's gender expectation that dancing is for girls. Billy dances throughout the film despite what his disapproving father says.

The infectious physicality and energy of the dance sequences which are captured using long shots, represent a sense of freedom. The long shots not only allow responders to engage with Billy's dancing but they also show how Billy relates with his environment; his world. Billy's world revolves around dance. Billy's gestures, expressing anger and frustration are also rhythmic and dance like. For example, in the scene where the Elliot family finds out about the audition and bans him from dancing, Billy runs out of the house. There he begins to pull his face and stamp his feet but this too, turns into an expressive dance sequence.

Much of the sound track is by T. Rex who had many hits in the seventies. T. Rex is an English Glam Rock group led by the creative direction of guitarist/vocalist Marc Bolan. The band often performed with heavy make up, sequined costumes teamed with a feather boa and matching platform shoes. The band were still regarded to be popular within the youth culture of the 80s. Glam Rock artists were not afraid to express themselves through their dress as well as their music. The sound track, therefore, transcends gendered stereotypes and reinforces a key theme.

As the height of T-Rex's popularity was in the seventies, it is assumed that the music belonged to Tony. Tony had some creative influence over his little brother. Billy liked to play Tony's records. While dance is a key aspect, the Director, Stephen Daldry, says that the movie is more than the story of a boy who wants to dance. *Billy Elliot* "is a film that celebrates the human spirit[2]". Thus Dance is important not in itself but for what it offers Billy Elliot; a means for self discovery.

Growing up

The film centres on Billy growing up amidst the hardship of family and societal turmoil caused by the miners' strike. Daldry stated, "I don't think it's a film about dance...I think it is a film about... leaving your family and the bittersweet element of growing out and growing up and moving on."[3] This quote links well to your elective topic. Billy grows into a new society, the world of professional dance. In the letter Billy's mother wrote to him, she tells him to be true to himself. Billy heeds this advice and remains true to his passion while growing up.

---

2   Allen, Jamie (2000) 'Billy Elliot' leaps into theatres, www.cnn.com/2000/SHOWBIZ/Movies/10/12/billy.elliot/
3   Ibid

© Five Senses Education Pty Ltd

Billy is not the only character in the film that grows up. Michael is also seen growing up throughout the film. He also had to face the barriers Billy faced including the socioeconomic problems caused by the miners' strike and the community's beliefs about what constituted appropriate behaviour for girls and boys. Michael was brave enough to admit his sexuality to his best friend. Evidence of Michael growing up is seen in Billy's big night where Michael was watching the performance with his partner. The character is wearing a flamboyant headdress as part of his costume. Like Billy, Michael was true to himself.

Adults can grow too. Jacky Elliot deals with the death of his wife which has forced him to raise their two sons on his own. In accepting his son's passion for dance, he develops a closer relationship with him. This can be seen through juxtaposition of the scene of Jacky and Billy joking around after they have received the good news of the letter and Jacky's earlier displeasure. The framing of the latter scene highlights the closeness of father and son. The natural lighting of the letter opening scene also creates a positive atmosphere suggesting that this is a new day for Billy and his father.

Gender Identity

Gender is defined as the cultural construction of femininity or masculinity; the notion of the appropriate behaviour for either sex. It includes everything a person does, from the clothes they wear and the job that they have, to their choice of recreational activities such as ballet. An individual may be male but have feminine preferences, according to what their society regards as "female". The contrary is true where a female may also display preferences for activities thought typically "male". Gender is distinct from sex, which is the biological difference between males and females. Gender, therefore, can, in part, describe the way in which masculinity and femininity serve to maintain the status quo in society. For example, the prevailing belief of the society around which *Billy Elliot* is set, is that ballet is for girls and that boys should play football or wrestle. The film presents a counter argument, advocating that boys can also dance and that society should not be limited to stereotypes. Thus, the film offers a message of transition, highlighting restrictions brought by adherence to stereotypes.

The character of Michael functions as an alternative to the heterosexual protagonist. Throughout the film, Michael displays feminine attributes which Billy accepts with an open heart. Michael seems to have a crush on his best friend who accepts him as he is but Billy does not reciprocate those feelings. The film offers non-judgemental values which operate on forgiveness and tolerance.

LANGUAGE OF FILM

By now you should be familiar with the devices that create meaning within film. Remember, for this module and elective, you are to explore how transitions have been represented through the language of film. Film is a visual language. Use the general film glossary at the beginning of this study guide. It is important to use terminology from the glossary and specific reference to the film in your responding and composing. Some of the main Language of Film features to consider are:

- Structure
- Production design and Mise-en-scène
- Framing
- Music and Lighting
- Editing, including camera shots and angles

Some of these are explored in greater detail in the following sub-sections -

Structure

The structure and sequence of this film conform to a regular narrative arc. The orientation is established early in the film. The historical and social context is developed in the scenes, Main Titles and A Disgrace in the Gloves. The complication is Billy's struggle, against the expectations of his family and community, in order to fulfil his dream to become a professional dancer. There are many heart breaking moments that lead to the climax of the audition, interview and acceptance letter. The dance of defiance is a hinge event that changes the course of the narrative. The denouement is the excitement of adult Billy's first leap as a principal ballet dancer.

Production design

The location of the production is central to the narrative. The mining town is an important aspect of the setting within the greater mise-en-scène. Many of the scenes are shot outside on location and not subject to the technological marvels of modern studios. Stephen Daldry set the fictional mining town of Everington in the real Easington where many of the locals still held strong feelings about the strike. The bleak industrial buildings and metallic structures provide a realistic backdrop to the action and actually visualise the toughness of the working class mining community. The setting of the scene, A Ghost Story is the impressive Middlesbrough's transporter bridge.

Framing

Framing is another filmic device which helps portray the relationships characters have with each other and with their environment. Long shots combined with high camera angles are often used to portray the protagonist feeling overwhelmed by their situation. An example is when Jacky and Billy Elliot step into the Royal Ballet School in London. The aerial long shot depicts the unfamiliarity of this new world. The marble interior of the building engulfs the figure suggesting that they have no control over this environment. If fact, they are now subject to the rules and value systems of the elite world of the Royal Ballet School. Long shots are also used to portray contrasting expressions of freedom where the long shots of Billy dancing are also juxtaposed with the shot sized used to frame Billy trapped within Everington. When Jacky Elliot accepts that his son is going to become a dancer, the developing relationship between father and son is portrayed using medium close ups. The medium close ups suggest a sense of intimacy that has evolved since Jacky has widened his gender based value systems.

Walls are also used as framing devices to symbolise the restrictions preventing Billy from fulfilling his dream. An example where this occurs is in the scene, the Chance to Dance. Once Billy is told that he can no longer dance, he is shown in a dance sequence to be taking his frustrations out by dancing into the wall. The first wall he dances into is the brick, red wall of his own house. The framing of this wall from a high camera angle presents the wall as an ominous, almost insurmountable obstacle.

Editing

The editor decides how long the shot will be and how transitions between shots are made. Editing has an important function in creating the pace and rhythm of the film. Many of the dance sequences incorporate rhythmic editing when the transitions between shots are in time to the beats of the musical sound track. Fast paced editing enhances the emotional intensity of the dance sequences. This is seen in the dance sequence after Billy misses out on the Newcastle audition due to Tony's incarceration. The argument between Tony and Mrs Wilkinson is edited rhythmically to the song 'Town Called Malice.' Not only do the lyrics of the song reinforce the animosity that Tony holds, the quick transitions of the rhythmic editing is also symbolic of Billy's confusion over his desire to dance and his family responsibilities.

Mise-en-scène

Mise-en-scène refers to the deliberate composition of a frame. It involves everything that is put in the frame such as lighting, costume, make-up, props and the physical movement of the figures. Lighting has a key role in creating atmosphere within a film. The dull overcast light of the scene where Billy visits his mother's grave with his grandmother adds to the sad nostalgic mood. On the other hand, the bright naturalistic lighting at the same setting when Billy revisits his mother's grave with his father creates a happy atmosphere between the now close father and son. *Low-key lighting* is used to enhance the feeling of suspense when Billy enters his first private ballet lesson with Mrs Wilkinson in the boxing club. This lighting emphasises Billy's shadow, as he hesitantly enters the club. *Backlighting* is also used in this scene around the figure of Mrs Wilkinson. She is in silhouette at the beginning of this scene. This also makes her look mysterious suggesting that Billy is unsure of what she expects.

The costumes and props reinforce the character types. The Elliot family wear what is expected of a middle class family from northern England in the mid 1980s, faced with economic difficulties. The colour of their clothes is generally restricted to a dark palette based upon navy and the dark blue of denims. Although Michael wears a similar costume to Billy, his costume is a reflection of his growth and development as he experiments with his sexuality. The dress that we see him try on is a bright green colour. This suggests that he does not have any negative feelings about what he is wearing. Rather, he sees explorations into cross dressing as fun.

When we first see Mr Wilkinson he is holding a glass filled with what we assume to be alcohol. This immediately signifies to the audience that he is associated with drink and it is later revealed by his daughter that he is an alcoholic. Mrs Wilkinson's cigarettes indicate that she is not really focused on teaching her ballet lessons because she is too busy lighting her cigarettes to pay close attention to what her students are performing.

ESSAY QUESTION

Read the question below carefully and then examine the essay outline on the following pages. Try to develop your essay along the suggested lines. You should also develop strategies to answer questions which are not essay based.

A list of differing response types is given at the end of the sample essay. Look at these. You should be familiar with most of them. Try to practise them when you can and develop your writing skills.

Essay Question

Explore the ways individuals in texts transition into new phases of life and social contexts. What are the results or consequences of such transitions?

Refer closely to your prescribed text and one related text.

THE ESSAY FORM

The essay has been the subject of numerous texts and you should have the basic form well in hand. As teachers, the point we would emphasise would be to link the paragraphs both to each other and back to your argument (which should directly respond to the question). Of course, ensure your argument is logical and sustained.

Make sure you use specific examples and that your quotes are accurate. To ensure that you respond to the question make sure you plan carefully and are sure what relevant point each paragraph is making. It is solid technique to actually 'tie up' each point by explicitly coming back to the question.

When composing an essay the basic conventions of the form are:

- State your argument, outline the points to be addressed and perhaps have a brief definition.

$\downarrow$

A solid structure for each paragraph is:
- Topic sentence (the main idea and its link to the previous paragraph/argument)
- Explanation / discussion of the point including links between texts if applicable.
- Detailed evidence (Close textual reference- quotes, incidents and technique discussion.)
- Tie up by restating the point's relevance to argument / question

$\downarrow$

- Summary of points
- Final sentence that restates your argument

As well as this basic structure you will need to focus on:

Audience – for the essay the audience must be considered formal unless specifically stated otherwise. Your language must reflect the audience. This gives you the opportunity to use the jargon and vocabulary you have learnt in English. For the audience ensure your introduction is clear and has impact. Avoid slang or colloquial language including contractions (like doesn't, eg. etc).

Purpose – the purpose of the essay is to answer the question. The examiner evaluates how well you can make an argument and understand the module's issues and its text(s). An essay is solidly structured so its composer can analyse ideas. This is where you earn marks. It does not retell the story or state the obvious.

Communication – Take a few minutes to plan the essay. If you rush into your answer it is almost certain you will not make the most of the given forty minutes to show all you know about the question. More likely you will include irrelevant details that do not gain you marks but waste your precious time. Remember, an essay is formal so do not do the following: story-tell, list and number points, misquote, use slang or colloquial language, be vague, use non sentences or fail to address the question.

ESSAY

Billy Elliot

In answering this question, it is important to consider the rubric.

In this elective, students explore and analyse a variety of texts that portray the ways in which individuals experience transitions into *new phases of life* **and** *social contexts.*

'New phases of life' may include changes for the young, middle aged and elderly. New 'social contexts' could involve starting school, moving from a family home to a nursing home, migrating or returning, remarrying, changing employment, retiring, becoming terminally ill, getting a disease or an illness such as dementia or travelling.

These transitions may be challenging, confronting, exciting or transformative and may result in growth, change and a range of consequences for the individual and others.

This section of the rubric considers the effects and results of the transition.

Through exploring their prescribed text and other related texts of their own choosing, students consider how transitions can result in new knowledge and ideas, shifts in attitudes and beliefs, and a deepened understanding of the self and others. Students respond to and compose a range

of texts that expand our understanding of the experience of venturing into new worlds.

A few notes about the question:

- Remember the actual question is asking you about the representation of how individuals make transitions and the effects.
- The question is to point you in the right direction. Define terms carefully.
- It is important you take note of the ideas the question raises and check your response does address them. In other words ANSWER THE QUESTION
- Take care you examine the prescribed text closely. This elective is Exploring Transitions and you are required to discuss this. Make good use of the rubric to direct you.

You MUST have quotations and textual references to demonstrate knowledge and understanding of your prescribed text and related material.

PLAN: Don't even think about starting without one!

Introduce... The director, film and other related texts you are using in the response Definition and Argument: Explanation of transition-growth and change, new phases and social contexts - results seen to be same as motivations for protagonist; to transform, for self-discovery.	Let the marker know what text(s) you are discussing. It is good to start with your definition but it could have come in the first paragraph of the body. You MUST state your argument in response to the question and the points you will cover. It is a good idea to respond to the to the quote in the introduction.

↓

Idea 1- Transitions experienced for key protagonists in prescribed and related texts. ▪ Explain the idea ▪ Where and how it is shown in the prescribed text and related material ▪ Here you will give specific examples and show how techniques reveal transition, growth and change. **Idea 2-** Results and consequences of the transitions are explored. ▪ where and how shown in the Prescribed text and related material? Here you will give specific examples and show how techniques reveal the results and consequences - could also be paralleled to motivations.	Two/three ideas are usually enough as you can explore them in detail. Use topic sentences to introduce each idea. Topic sentences are very important as they clarify your argument for the reader. You can integrate your points or deal with texts separately. Some say 60% prescribed material and 40% related material but others say equal treatment of texts in essays. The syllabus notes the related should supplement the prescribed text.

↓

▪ Summary of two key ideas ▪ Final sentence that restates your argument	Use quotes and textual references from the prescribed text and related material. A sophisticated response will compare and contrast the ideas between the prescribed text and related material

ESSAY RESPONSE

Explore the ways individuals in texts transition into new phases of life and social contexts. What are the results or consequences of such transitions?

Transitions revolve around growth and change. 'New phases of life' may include physical and emotional changes for the young, middle aged and elderly. New 'social contexts' often involve leaving security or expectations behind and venturing forth into a new social context. Such experiences inevitably bring about positive or negative consequences for the individual undergoing change. The film *Billy Elliot*, (2000) directed by Stephen Daldry explores personal transition through strong characterisation and narrative involving juxtaposition of values. Billy, at the start of the text, is a child, expected to conform to societal values. At the conclusion he is an adult fulfilling his dreams, having challenged the gender and class stereotypes offered by his society. Similarly, Shaun Tan's *The Red Tree* explores the concept of transition. It is, however, through a different visual form, that of a picture book. Words and illustrations form the narrative which focuses on symbolism to trace an individual's quest for self worth and the confidence to move into society. Both characters achieve self fulfilment, a sense of identity and self worth but it is Billy Elliot who physically escapes his confining context. Tan's protagonist does not physically transition to a new social context but rather, learns to see her old context in a new light. The results are closely linked to the motivation to transition and involve a desire to overcome confining situations.

In the film, setting is closely linked to values and it is the limiting values of his childhood from which Billy wishes to escape. *Billy*

Elliot, is set in England during the context of the miners' strike of 1984. It examines the story of one boy's dream to become a professional dancer. The character of Billy Elliot transitions. He develops from a mining town lad to become a principal London ballet dancer. The film explores his growing up in a town where he has struggled against the gendered expectations of his working class community and the impoverished socioeconomic situation of his family due to the miners' strike. He transitions into the wider world when he successfully auditions for the London ballet.

The film's setting and mise-en-scène visually symbolise the obstacles the protagonist had to face. For example, in the scene where Mrs Wilkinson is taking Billy on an excursion over the Middlesborough transporter bridge, she tells him of the story of the famous ballet, *Swan Lake*. The long shot of the tremendous steel structure overwhelms the two characters. The setting represents how Billy felt emotionally. He was overwhelmed by his situation; having private dance lessons in secret, in preparation for the Royal Ballet School. Another scene which incorporates the idea that Billy is subjugated by his environment is when he undertakes the journey to London for his audition. The aerial long shots of Billy and Jacky Elliot also suggest that they are nervous about being in this strange new world.

The framing of Billy's working class neighbourhood also conveys a sense that he is closed in by his context. The miners' strike has produced a tight knit community, reflected in the closed in houses in the street where Billy lives. Therefore, framing is an important filmic device used to represent obstacles and to highlight his need to transition. Conversely, the framing of the dance sequences illustrate the liberation and freedom Billy feels while he is dancing.

The setting of the greater struggle of the miners' strike symbolically parallels the conflict occurring within the Elliot household. Billy's mother has recently passed away. Billy has the responsibility to take care of his aging maternal grandmother while seeking a means of self-expression through dance. Billy faces conflict with his father Jacky and stubborn brother Tony over his desire to dance. It is expected that Billy becomes a boxer and miner like his father and his father's father. This sport is valued by his traditional society as being a valid masculine pathway. Ballet, on the other hand, was ideologically held as a feminine pastime. Billy navigates this value laden, small town terrain and emerges personally fulfilled, as a successful principal dancer in a wider world.

The Red Tree, composed by Shaun Tan, also portrays a young protagonist struggling to grow up and move into the world. Unlike Billy, the red haired girl does not move physically. Rather, she is moved by her imagined environment and changed attitude. It is not until the end of the text that the unnamed red headed young girl actually moves into the world. The girl does not physically move to the city or a new part of the world, rather her transition is an inner, personal rather than physical journey. For Billy Elliot, it is both a personal and physical journey. The majority of the story of *The Red Tree* is the visualisation of the process of emotional self-discovery. The world that is depicted in the picture book is from the young girl's imagination of how she perceives her life.

Tan uses highly stylised surreal images to represent the girl's world. In one image, the girl believes that she has no choice over her future. The text states, "Terrible fates are inevitable" (Tan, 2003:19) and the accompanying image presents a game board, representing chance. The image is also framed in a long shot where the setting engulfs the protagonist. The pathway on which the girl is walking resembles squares. Just like the industrial images contained within *Billy Elliot*, the salient image of the building is an ominous metallic monstrosity which dwarfs the girl. In order for her to complete the game she will have to pass this building. The other brick buildings also convey a sense that she too is closed in by her surroundings. The young girl is carrying a large dice that symbolises life is a game but the outcome is inevitable as all of the sides have six on them.

Billy Elliot makes his move into the world through dance. After failing in the boxing ring, Billy's interest in dance grew after observing a ballet class taught by the chain smoking Mrs Wilkinson. It was she who dared him to take off the blue boxing boots, to replace them with ballet slippers. Thus, juxtaposition is a key technique to reveal transition. Mrs Wilkinson recognised Billy's natural talent, a talent that would take him to the Royal Ballet School, London.

Not only does dance provide a means for Billy to be true to himself, it is also a means of liberation, physically and emotionally. Billy physically transitions when he journeys to London to take part in the audition. It is there he remains to become the fine dancer of Billy's Big Night. Billy expresses himself through dance; it is a means where he can vent his frustration, grief and anger caused by his personal context. Dance is used metaphorically to represent the freedom of moving and transitioning beyond the confines of set contexts in order to discover personal identity.

The framing of the dance sequences also represent freedom. For example in the scene, the Chance to Dance, where the Elliot family finds out about the audition, Billy storms out of the house angry over the decision that he can no longer be a dancer. The gestures that the character makes, pulling his face and stomping his feet, soon transform to become an infectious physical dance sequence. The shot size is a long shot that not only represents the freedom felt while Billy dances but also illustrates the relationship that the character has with his environment. The reoccurring motif is also explored in this scene through the dance movements. Billy is seen scraping his hands over his back wall to dance down the street straight into the corrugated iron wall that is blocking his way. The wall symbolises the obstacles that Billy has to go overcome in the process of transitioning.

Conversely, the girl of *The Red Tree* makes her journey into the world not through the physicality of dance but through the internal method of using her imagination. Her imagination creates a world of fantasy and make believe, which allows her to cope with her situation. The image of the girl drawing a self-portrait on a wall suggests that she is attempting to create the woman she wants to become but she does not know what she wants to be when she grows up. The supporting text proclaims, "sometimes you just don't know...who you are meant to be" (Tan, 2003:20-22). She feels empty. This is demonstrated through the visual language of the painting she is creating on the wall. The painting is mere outline, devoid of colour. The painting has negative connotations because it is not complete. The girl is in control over her own image, which does suggest that there is hope. She can decide upon the colours that she wants to paint in. Therefore, she is in control of her own destiny.

Shaun Tan's text uses the reoccurring motif of a solitary leaf that comes from the red tree to symbolise change. The leaf is placed in the images throughout the entire text in a puzzle-like fashion. The red tree is symbolic of the positive forces that help an individual to achieve success through transition. Just as the leaves are scattered throughout the narrative, so too are these positive forces. It is up to the reader to find them.

The obstacles the unnamed girl faces in her transition are her own negative perceptions of her self and her environment. She believes that she is alone in the world and feels overwhelmed by her circumstances. An example of the figure feeling overwhelmed by her context is on page four. The text states "...darkness overcomes you" (Tan, 2003:4). The image is an extreme long shot of the girl walking through an urban neighbourhood. The figure's body language suggests she is depressed. She is walking with her head hung low, avoiding eye contact with the world around her. This reinforces the fact that the girl is not interacting with her physical surroundings. Rather, she is drawn within the limitations of her own psyche.

The girl is positioned in the background within the shadow, which reinforces the idea that she is confounded by the situation of her own creation. She is depicted as being literally engulfed by the surrounding buildings. The girl is also not aware of the giant fish coming up behind her. The fish signifies darkness judging from its dull colours. It is a Biblical allusion to leviathan whale that swallowed men whole. Mrs Wilkinson offered Billy an alternative, a lifeline from which to escape his stifling environment. The red haired girl has only herself.

The picture book is circular in structure. It ends in the place where the story began, the girl's bedroom. The colour red is symbolic of blood that provides us with life but we need to live our life with the intensity and passion that this colour evokes. The red tree is fully formed in the last frame of the text. The red tree stands out in the dark room where the light streaming in from the doorway acts as a vector leading to the tree which is positioned in the foreground of the image. The young girl has moved into the world and has grown as a consequence but it was not until she realised that all the things that she was looking for were right in front of her. She had access to them to begin with.

Billy Elliot and *The Red Tree* use the visual language of film and picture book respectively to represent the emotional growth, change and establishment of identity of two unique individuals. While the film uses a strong narrative arc, setting and characterisation to do so, the picture book relies more on symbolism. Billy Elliot is a figure who, despite many obstacles, moves into the world finding self-expression in dance. The red haired girl in *The Red Tree* on the other hand is moved by changes to her personal perspectives. For both characters, the transitions are overwhelmingly positive and contribute to greater self worth and stronger concepts of self-identity. Growth and change are two positive outcomes although the process of transition was, for both protagonists, fraught with obstacles of either their own making or due to the values of others. Both are able to make significant contributions to a wider society once they have established their own identity. Billy does this through a changed social context, the red-haired girl does not change her social context but changes her attitudes and perspectives.

REFERENCES

Daldry, Stephen (2000) *Billy Elliot*, Working Title Films

Tan, Shaun (2003) *The Red Tree*, Lothian Books: South Melbourne.

OTHER TYPES OF RESPONSES

It is crucial students realise that their responses in the examination, class and assessment tasks will NOT always be an essay. This page is designed to give guidance with the different types of responses which are now required.

The response types covered in the exam may include some of the following:

- Writing in a role
- Journal/Diary Entry
- Brochure
- Point of view
- Radio interview
- Television interview
- Letter
- Feature article
- Speech
- Report

Students should also familiarise themselves with these types of responses and be able to write effectively in them. You should practise each one at some stage of your HSC year.

For a comprehensive explanation of each of these writing forms with examples using the prescribed HSC texts see:

Pattinson, Bruce and Suzan, *Success in HSC Standard English: A Practical Guide for Senior Students*

Pattinson, Bruce and Suzan, *Success in HSC Advanced English: A Practical Guide for Senior Students*

OTHER QUESTIONS

1. As an expert in the field, you have been invited to speak to a group of HSC students on the topic of Exploring Transitions.

   Write the speech referring to the prescribed text and one other piece of related material.

2. You have been invited to compose a brooklet for grade six students who are making the transition to High School. The brochure must explore the representation of the theme growing up.

   Compose the brochure referring to the prescribed text and other related material.

3. Knowledge, attitudes and belief systems are particular to specific areas of society. Do you agree?

   You are to compose a feature article for *The Sydney Morning Herald* outlining the difficulties adolescents have growing up.

   Compose the feature article referring to your prescribed text and other related material.

4. Stephen Daldry has been invited to appear on a talk back radio show to discuss his film and its suitability for this HSC module and elective. Compose the radio interview referring to the prescribed text and one other related text of your own choosing.

ANNOTATED GUIDE TO RELATED MATERIAL

There are many suitable related texts. Remember you are looking for something that will enable you to discuss the techniques used to represent how individuals grow up, move and go through transitions in order to enter new phrases of life within society.

Texts with a clear vision of a transition are most useful as you can analyse how that person's transition is being represented. *Billy Elliot* is a feature film, so it may be a good idea for you to have related texts that are within other forms and genres so you can compare and contrast a variety of techniques.

With all related texts, it is best to find your own. Examiners love to see students show that they have though about related texts and how they link to the prescribed text as well as to the module and elective. Be sure to focus closely on how transition is represented through techniques.

The following are additional suggestions.

Looking for Alibrandi   Novel

Melina Marchetta   Penguin, 1992

ISBN 0 14 036046 8

Josephine Alibrandi is a girl of Italian Australian background in her last year of school. She is a scholarship girl at an exclusive school and feels out of step with most of the other students whom she sees as having perfect lives due to their money and position.

Josephine feels constrained by her Italian family and longs for her 'emancipation' from them. Over the course of the year, she has experiences which shape her. She meets her father and develops a relationship with him, she has a relationship with a boy from the local high school and she loses a friend to suicide. All of these experiences help her to forge a stronger identity and to be more ready to transition into a more mature person. She realises that money and position are no guarantee of a perfect life and that she is in charge of her own destiny.

My Dog, (2002)   Picture Book

Written by John Heffernan,   Illustrated by Andrew McLean

Ashton Scholastic

Summary

My Dog is an award winning picture book that tells the story of a young boy, Alija's, growth and development during the Bosnian war. Alija lived peacefully with his family in the little town of Liztar. He often helped his father who was a baker. One day while delivering bread for his father, he came across an elderly man who was walking through the town square followed by his little dog. When Alija offered the seated man some bread to eat, he realised that the elderly man was dead. After the man was buried the little dog followed Alija home. Alija adopted the dog who soon became his best friend.

War was coming closer to his village. His grandmother and younger sister were sent to safety. When the soldiers came Alija was sent also, with his mother, but soldiers came and took his mother away. Now separated from his family, the little dog is his only companion. The story ends with Alija in the company of a friendly man who takes him in to live with his daughter's family. Alija is still waiting for his family with the dog at his side.

My Dog was judged Book of the Year for Young Reader when published and has also won the Honour Book prize in the Picture Book section of the Children's Book Council of Australia awards.

Analysis

The picture book uses both written and visual language to represent the theme of Exploring Transitions in the specific context of war. Therefore, your analysis should focus on both written and visual techniques. Similar to the point-of-view shots used in *Billy Elliot*, many of the images in this book are from the young protagonist's point-of-view. This is his world that is narrated with a child like voice; therefore the atrocities of the war are hidden within the subtext. It is not until the end of the text that you realise that Heffernan dedicated the book to the victims of ethnic cleansing. The consequences of war are the major obstacles that the protagonist goes through in his transition to become an adult. These include death, separation and unconditional love. The value systems that are presented are those concerning the validity of such violent conflict.

The images are composed using sketches and watercolours. The concept of growth and development is represented and symbolised by the many images of roads. The roads act as vectors that lead the responder in the direction that the protagonist is moving but the destination is unclear. This suggests that Alija's future is uncertain. Uncertainty is also represented by the use of dark colours within the images. Dark shadows are used to represent the negative associations of the soldiers and the shadows of the refugees who are fleeing from the violence and bloodshed.

What is the matter with Mary Jane? (1996)

Wendy Harmer & Sancia Robinson

Currency Press Ltd

Summary

What is the matter with Mary Jane? is Sancia Robinson's real life story about growing up with an eating disorder. It presents a realistic image about what it is to live with this condition as a young woman and how the same sense of insecurity has progressed into her thirties. The actor speaks to the audience throughout the entire performance.

Analysis

The play is a monodrama, which means that there is only one actor who is on stage throughout the entire performance. Although one actor is on stage, other characters are explored in the dramatic situation. Not only is this demanding for the actor but it also creates a sense of intimacy between performer and audience. This is highlighted by the fact that this is the actor's real life experience. The use of the individual voice also allows the representation of the character to be more effective. Your analysis should consider how this text would be performed on stage and how this performance would affect the audience. To do this you will need to envisage how the script should be performed as well as focusing on the mise-en-scène of the stage setting.

The play is divided into eleven sections that provide the audience with some idea about the obsessive nature of eating disorders. Dark humour is used to represent the process of dealing with the obstacle of having anorexia. The protagonist uses eating disorders as a means of creating her own identity. A mirror is used symbolically throughout the performance, where the mirror is actually the performer looking at the audience. This suggests that what the girl sees is not real but a figment of her distorted imagination. *What is the matter with Mary Jane?* suggests that in order to progress and transition, we often need to accept our limitations which we once thought were obstacles.

OTHER RELATED MATERIAL

- **A Christmas Carol** by Charles Dickens. Novel and Film. *A Christmas Carol* is a classic Victorian tale, set in England and written by Charles Dickens. It tells of Ebenezer Scrooge and his transformation of heart after supernatural visits. Scrooge becomes a more generous hearted person and less miserly and negative after his experiences.

- **Bend It Like Beckham** Directed by Gurinder Chadra. 2002. Film. A young British Indian girl succeeds in playing soccer against the wishes of her conservative family and eventually wins a sports scholarship in America.

- **Bridal Train** Written and performed by The Waifs. 2004. The song is about women leaving their home of Western Australia to marry American sailors.

- **'Butterfly'** John Tranter. Poem. In this poem a young woman keeps moving into new situations or new worlds, seeking something elusive.

- **Cinema Paradiso** Directed by Guiseppe Tornatore. 1989. Film. A young boy, Toto's, passage to manhood. Alfredo, the projectionist at the theatre is an important mentor to him.

- **Curious Case of Benjamin Button** 2008. Film. Directed by David Finche. Rather than age, the reverse happens in the case of Benjamin Button.

- **Dead Poet's Society** Directed by Peter Weir. 1989. Film. A class of boys are inspired by the teacher to break tradition and strive for their dreams.

- **Father and Son** Cat Stephens/Yusuf Islam. Song about changing roles of father and son. The life of the songwriter also demonstrates transition.

- **Finding Forrester** Directed by Gus Van Sant. 2000. Film. A teenager, Jamal, is inspired by a recluse, Forrester and both escape their difficulties and embrace the opportunities before them.

- **Forrest Gump** Directed by Robert Zemeckis. This film explores one man's extraordinary journey through life and some significant historical moments.

- **Longtime Gone** Dixie Chicks Song. 202http://www.lyricsfreak.com/d/dixie+chicks/long+time+gone_20041016.html

- **Mao's Last Dancer** Li Cunxin. Penguin, 2003. A young boy moves beyond an impoverished background and to international success through ballet school. This is available as a film and Picture Book also.

- **My Beautiful Broken Brain** Documentary. https://www.youtube.com/watch?v=imsJLAM42jw. A documentary on a young woman and the changes that came after a stroke.

- **My Brother Jack** by George Johnson, 1964. Novel. This journey to self-realisation follows the lives of two brothers born and raised in the Melbourne suburbs. The younger brother is Davy who enjoys reading and the older brother is Jack – the solid reliable bloke.

- **The Arrival** Shaun Tan. Lothian, 2006. Picture book. This depicts the difficulties and fears immigrants must overcome upon their arrival in a new country.

- **The Circle Game** performed by Joni Mitchell. A song about the seasons of life.

- **The Picture of Dorian Gray** by Oscar Wilde. Novel and Film Dorian Gray sells his soul and the result is ageless beauty. While the portrait of Dorian transforms, his appearance does not. Until...

- **The Red Tree, Lothian Books:** South Melbourne. Picture Book. Tan, Shaun (2003)

- **Transparent.** http://www.npr.org/2014/09/26/351489758/TV Series. In *Transparent* a seventy year old divorced dad becomes a woman.

- **Window.** Illustrated by Jeanie Baker. This picture book uses the central image of a window on each page and presents the changes observed by the characters.